MW00579606

To my Frien...

Peace & Grace !
Strength & Honor .

BUSINESS BY THE BOOK

BUSINESS
BY
THE BOOK

LEADERSHIP AND MANAGEMENT PRINCIPLES
FROM THE LIFE OF CHRIST

DR. JOHN A. KING

Business By The Book — Leadership And Management Principles from the Life of Christ
© Dr. John A. King 2006

Website: www.imnonline.org
Email: info@imnonline.org

USA Head Office
Tel: +1 817 993 0047
Fax: +1 817 674 6100
PO Box 827, Roanoke, TX 76262, USA

Scripture quotations are taken from the Holy Bible, New International Version. NIV. Copyright © 1973, 1978, 1984 by International Bible Society. New King James Version. Copyright © 1988, Thomas Nelson, Inc. New Living Translation. Copyright © 1197 Tyndale House Publishers, Inc.

COIN DISPLAYED ON THE COVER:
Tiberius Caesar Augustus — Reign: 14 - 37 Born: November 16, 42 BC Died: March 16 AD 37 Born Tiberius Claudius Nero, he was the second Roman Emperor, from the death of Augustus in AD 14 until his own death in 37. Tiberius was by birth a Claudian, son of Tiberius Nero and Livia. Tiberius deserves recognition as one of Rome's greatest generals, whose campaigns in Pannonia, Illyricum, Rhaetia and Germany laid the foundations for the northern frontier. Also, Tiberius Caesar Augustus ruled during the time of Christ.

All rights reserved. This book or parts thereof may not be reproduced in any form, stored in a retrieval system, or transmitted in any form or by any means — electronic, mechanical, photocopy, recorder, carrier pigeon or even a rock with paper attached by a piece of string! (or otherwise) — without prior permission of the publisher. If you are even reading this, it means you are thinking about flogging it, so why don't you drop me an email and I can see how I can help. Hey, don't scan it! I'll probably just email you the text. So sit back, have a coffee and drop me a note — God rewards the righteous and sends plagues of fleas into the armpits of those who infringe copyright!

Design by Jakki Parker

Typeset Garamond 12pt

Printed by Lightning Source Inc.

ISBN 7774590633

$\mathscr{D}$EDICATION

DR. ED COLE & THE MEN OF IMN
On every page are quotes and thoughts that are not mine but
yours. I write them as mine because I live them as mine;
but I acknowledge them as 'ours'.

AS DR. COLE TAUGHT US:
'The first time, I'll quote you.
The second time, I'll say a friend once told me;
The third time "As I have always said..."'

Miss you Doctor… We all do.

$\mathcal{A}$CKNOWLEDGEMENTS

In just a few short years we have grown from a small start up in
Australia to an international organization based in the USA
that is touching people all over the world.

No race is ever won without the support of those that know
you best. No man has ever achieved anything without
the encouragement of a friend.

TO JIM HALEK & JOHN BINKLEY
When I thought I couldn't you told me I could.

RANCE & LARHEA SMITH AND ERIK KUDLIS
It would have been impossible if you did not stand by us.

This fruit I add to your account, not mine.

Thank you

Contents

CONTENTS

Principles Of Longevity

$\mathcal{I}$NTRODUCTION

"The Truth shall make you free."
John 8:32

$\mathcal{A}$ll truth is transferable, as long as it is truth. As Leaders we tend to compartmentalize our lives. Business Leadership, Man on Saturday, Church Leadership on Sunday. How asinine! Jesus Christ was not only a profound teacher, He was an incredible leader. If you want the best example of going from Good to Great or Build to Last, just look at the enormous impact the followers of Christ are still having 2000 years after He vacated the church. The reason? He taught truth.

Have you ever wondered how people can sit in church or business seminars for years, hear brilliant life-changing principles and then go out and do really dumb stuff? Truth is like soap: just having a bar does not affect you, and it is only in its application that its true working power is revealed.

All truth starts as information. It all really starts to work when it becomes a personal revelation, when it moves from the head to the heart. It is no longer a general principle — it is YOUR principle.

That's when it is starting to 'make' you free. But the real

test comes in the final phase. It has to go from information, to revelation, to application. Only after personal application can truth bring freedom.

I trust that you came to this book looking for more information. I trust you have come looking for time-tested truths that shall have an impact on your everyday life in a profound way.

Here's to Truth
And the ears that hear it,
The hearts that absorb it,
And the hands that apply it.

John King

PRINCIPLES FOR LIFE

NEVER FEAR THE WANT OF BUSINESS.
A MAN WHO QUALIFIES HIMSELF
WELL FOR HIS CALLING NEVER
FAILS OF EMPLOYMENT.

Thomas Jefferson

KNOW YOUR PURPOSE

"He steadfastly set His face to go to Jerusalem."

Luke 9:51

Jesus came to earth with a clear purpose in mind. He knew what He was called to do and He knew how this was going to be accomplished. Nothing deterred Him.

He was steadfast: His purpose was His passion and focus.

- A plan puts you in charge of your energies and activities.
- A plan means that you respond to circumstances, not react.
- A plan enables you to become productive and proactive.

Most people don't plan. I think of it this way; most people in life never stop to ask the second question. They spend their lives seeking the great 'what' but never stop to ask 'how.'

A vision is a dream with a plan attached.

You have to have more than just a good idea if you want to leave a legacy behind for those that follow on after you. To have a life purpose, a life goal is not only to know what you are supposed to do, but also to posses a clear strategy as to how to achieve it and then posses the tenacity to see it through.

Christ had all three of these components. He had the which, He had the how and He had the passion. The result of which is still being felt 2000 years later.

> MOST PEOPLE IN LIFE NEVER STOP TO ASK
> THE SECOND QUESTION — HOW?

DON'T PRAY FOR OPPORTUNITIES — PREPARE FOR THEM

"Work hard so God can approve you. Be a good worker."

2 Timothy 2:15

From the beginning of time, Jesus was being prepared for His role as Savior. When Jesus walked the earth, He spent 30 years having His character honed, walking out His destiny. He didn't have to pray for what was coming, He had to prepare for it.

Paul's second letter to Timothy urged his young protégé to "work hard, study, so that God can approve of you and so you won't be ashamed."

Don't get daunted by the thought of trying to be extraordinary. The only difference between an ordinary person and an extra-ordinary person is the extra. Just that little bit more. The difference between an extra-ordinary athlete and an ordinary athlete is 15 minutes more in the gym. It is just that little bit extra.

Winners are not those that never fail,
but those that never quit.

Failure to prepare is preparation for failure. For in preparation is proof:

* Proof of your willingness.
* Proof of your planning.
* Proof of your passion.
* Proof of your determination.
* Proof of your dedication.

> ## COME PREPARED FOR YOUR DESTINY,
> ## DON'T GO LOOKING FOR HANDOUTS, BUT
> ## PREPARE FOR OPPORTUNITIES.

*L*EADERSHIP IS NOT A DEMOCRACY

" For J also, am a man under authority."

Luke 7:8

In a day and age where leadership is by consensus and committee, the leadership style of Jesus Christ seems out of place. But Jesus was not trying to win a popularity contest; He was determined to fulfil His destiny and mandate on the earth.

One day a centurion came to him with a personal request. Christ offered to go with Him and help, but the centurion refused. In a sense he said "You are too big a man to deal with this personally. Command it and it shall be so, because all things are subject to you".

Jesus was a man under authority: He went about doing the will of the Father. In this scripture, we see that He admired the Centurion and his grasp and view of authority. In other parts of the New Testament, Jesus taught parables that showed the consequences of a disobedient servant. He clearly stated time and time again that a disciple was known by his ability to follow out the orders/commands he was given.

It was vitally important to Jesus that He had His team on the same side and going in the same direction. There was no room for debate about how things were going to happen. When Peter, one of Jesus' closest friends, tried to challenge His leadership and get Jesus to change His game plan (Matt 10:23), he was quickly, quietly and firmly told otherwise.

The reason was that Jesus didn't have a choice on whether or not to follow through with the agreed plan; He was a man under authority: *"Not my will...but Yours be done."* Jesus was a man under authority with a greater love for His Father and what His Father wanted than the need to have consensus of the board and the popularity of His followers. He was a single-focused leader, with a great love and compassion for people and a determination to get it done... and He was prepared to pay whatever price was necessary in order to achieve His goal. He didn't mind discussions, He had no problem giving second chances, but when it came down to crunch time, you were either in or out...and you were personally responsible for that choice.

WHEN IT CAME DOWN TO CRUNCH TIME, YOU WERE EITHER IN OR OUT... AND YOU WERE PERSONALLY RESPONSIBLE FOR THAT CHOICE.

$\mathscr{P}$EOPLE LIVE ON VISION

"Man does not live on bread alone."

Luke 4:4

Jesus taught that people don't live on bread alone.

Over the years Beccy and I have been involved with many start-up projects. In the early days of any project there is great energy, great excitement, long hours and little money!

Not once in all my years was money ever a factor in people working for me. People wanted to get involved. In fact, they would take huge pay cuts to get involved. Once the vision caught their hearts, nothing was going to stand in their way.

Once inside and once committed, it was often years before we would see the return of our labors. We all made huge personal sacrifices to see the dream fulfilled.

WHAT SUSTAINED US?

▓ VISION – If you don't have one, you perish.

23

- VISION – If you lose sight of it, you will lose motivation and discipline.
- VISION – Without it, you stop marching forward and retreat to your past.
- VISION – A clear picture of where we are going and a clear understanding of the impact that what we are doing will have once we get there.

You have to make a Vision plan!

You have to:
- Write it down
- Discuss it
- Dream about it
- Strategize over it
- Keep it before you and your team

Remember, it is the reason that you are doing what you are doing. If you lose sight of the objective, if you lose sight of the end goal, you will very soon grow weary of doing good. Vision: It will sustain you... even when the bread is scarce.

> IT IS THE REASON FOR YOU DOING WHAT YOU ARE DOING. IT WILL SUSTAIN YOU, EVEN WHEN THE BREAD IS SCARCE.

EVERY TOMORROW HAS TWO HANDLES.
WE CAN TAKE HOLD OF IT BY THE
HANDLE OF ANXIETY, OR BY THE
HANDLE OF FAITH.

Author Unknown

*P*ERPETUAL DEVOTION TO WHAT A
MAN CALLS HIS BUSINESS IS ONLY TO BE
SUSTAINED BY PERPETUAL NEGLECT
OF MANY OTHER THINGS.

Robert Louis Stevenson

*T*IME OUT IS NOT A LUXURY, IT IS ESSENTIAL FOR LONGEVITY

" And when He had sent them away, He departed to the mountain to pray."

Mark 6:46

Jesus often took time out to reflect, recharge and refocus. With the busy demands of corporate or community leadership, it is essential to get away and get some 'head space.'

The catch cry of 'I don't have time' is not a reflection of your schedule, but of your poor time management skills. What does it profit you to gain the whole world and yet have your family, your health and your soul in tatters?

Jesus would take off to the mountains regularly, not for months at a time, but for hours or days at regular intervals. He would be un-contactable during these short periods to all but His very inner circle, and still with them, there were times when He was totally unavailable.

When I am talking of getting away, I mean no laptop, no phone, no pager, and no fax. I mean taking 36 - 48 hours once a month to disengage from the world and reengage with yourself and your family.

You may be called to live a life of sacrifice for your job, your visions, your passion, your calling, but your family is not a part of that sacrifice equation. Whatever is so pressing on Thursday will still be there Tuesday. To paraphrase: Paperwork we will have with us always, even to the end of the age...

> PAPER WORK WE WILL HAVE WITH US ALWAYS, EVEN TO THE END OF THE AGE...

STAY IN TOUCH WITH YOUR PEOPLE

"If anyone desires to be first, he shall be last of all and a servant of all."

Mark 9:35

Logan Smith said: *"When they come downstairs from their Ivory Towers, Idealists are very apt to walk straight into the gutter".*

All your ideas and all you budget cuts and all you new plans and all your new dreams have very real world implications.

- ✳ Will it work?
- ✳ Will they like it?
- ✳ Do they want it?
- ✳ Or are you answering questions that no one is asking?

People seem to forget that you have to sell your new product to someone other than the marketing department.

Jesus spent time with people outside of His circle constantly. Through His life, He deliberately made an effort to connect with people He didn't know. In fact, His connectedness was not so much a deliberate effort at a particular time as it was a constant part of His life.

If He was sitting by a well waiting for water, He took time to connect. Walking through a crowd, He connected. A man up a tree, He connected. Blind people, He connected. Rich city rulers, He connected. It was the people that He loved and the people that He came to connect with.

Jesus taught His team that the more they serve, the greater they would become. The higher up the corporate ladder you go, the easier the possibility of isolation becomes, so if you have to, force yourself to stay in touch with those that serve you and those you are called to serve.

Jesus always took time to listen, explain, show and encourage those His life and future were going to impact.

> THE MORE WE SERVE, JESUS SAID, THE GREATER WE BECOME.

$\mathscr{B}$E CAREFUL WHOM YOU CHOOSE AS A MENTOR

" $\mathscr{A}$ student is not above his teacher, nor a servant above his master. "

Matthew 10:24

Jesus said that the servant will never become greater than the master.

A great friend of mine, Ed Cole, would say: *"When we accept other men's philosophies that are rationalizations to their failures, then we accept their failures".* In short, you will never rise above the belief systems of your mentors.

But what you can do is choose who you submit to mentally. You need to ask yourself honestly: is this person, my mentor, everything and more that I ever want to be in every area of my life? Are they doing more than I ever want to do? Do I agree with what they say and the unsaid philosophies expressed in their lives? Would I be happy with only achieving 80% of what they achieve?

If you answer "yes" to all these questions — then you are getting great input for this stage of your life.

If your answer is no... then you have to find a new 'master', a new mentor, because you will never rise above the ceiling *you* have put in place by your chosen associations.

Now, I am not encouraging rebellion but personal responsibility. I am talking about your mentors, not your bosses or team leaders. I am talking of those whose philosophies you choose to submit to.

On a personal level, I have several mentors in different areas of my life — all of them the best there ever was in their chosen field. I am their student, they are my teachers. I willingly, actively, knowingly, submit to them. Some of them living, some of them dead. To be a student of history is to be a student of possibility. Don't limit yourself to the 'latest greatest' because there is nothing new under the sun. If I am going to submit myself to the teachings and input of a great man or woman — I want the original, and I want the best.

Search out history for the great voice of the past that can instruct, correct, and direct you in the way you should go. Jesus always quoted the great teachers of His day. He often talked about how He was committed to fulfilling their mandate, not destroying it. He felt He was a living extension of their thoughts, passions and ideas. He felt He had the opportunity to bring about all that they had ever started or dreamt about.

He could look back through the writings of His forefathers

and see their victories, their defeats, their successes and failures and from those writings He could draw and redraw the map for His own success.

What a sense of purpose! What mentors to follow!

Choose your mentors wisely, it will determine your future success.

> WHEN WE ACCEPT OTHER MEN'S PHILOSOPHIES THAT ARE RATIONALIZATIONS TO THEIR FAILURES WE ACCEPT THEIR FAILURES.

$\mathscr{M}$ OST OF US, SWIMMING AGAINST THE
TIDES OF TROUBLE THE WORLD KNOWS
NOTHING ABOUT, NEED ONLY A BIT OF
PRAISE OR ENCOURAGEMENT— AND
WE WILL MAKE THE GOAL.

Jerome P. Fleishman

$\mathcal{Y}$OU CAN ONLY LIVE IN ONE STATE OF MIND

"Therefore do not worry about tomorrow."

Matthew 6:33 - Matthew 7:2

Now is the only moment we have and the only one we can either control or enjoy.

As leaders we are constantly faced with a 'time displacement challenge.' I know it sounds a little like something off the Sci-Fi channel instead of the daily challenge of leaders. Yet because of the nature of who we are and what we do, we are constantly living in three states of mind — and that is impossible and unhealthy.

We try to straddle our yesterdays through constant reflection, our tomorrows with constant planning, and our todays with constant worry!

Jesus' advice is sound, so let's put it in context. He knew where He came from, where He was going, and what He had to do today to get it done.

In this passage of teaching relayed by His friend Matthew, Jesus wasn't copping out, what He was saying is that you have to have the ability to opt out of the stress and pressure of the 'what ifs' and 'what might have been.'

He says: First, concentrate on the big picture things, on the things of most importance to your life. If you seek first these things, everything else will fall into place.

Second, don't worry about what tomorrow will bring, but focus on today. Tomorrow will take care of itself if you give enough dedication to the preparation of today.

Finally don't judge others for what they have done in the past. Don't hold grudges and don't cast judgements. We are often too ready to judge others by their actions and ourselves by our intentions.

You can only live one day at a time, one breath at time — NOW is all we have and all we can be sure of, so don't let it pass you by. Live THIS moment passionately and your future will follow accordingly.

NOW IS THE ONLY MOMENT WE HAVE AND
THE ONLY ONE WE CAN EITHER
CONTROL OR ENJOY.

THERE IS NOTHING BETTER THAN
THE ENCOURAGEMENT OF A
GOOD FRIEND.

Katharine Butler Hathaway

PRINCIPLES OF LEADERSHIP

YOU DO NOT LEAD BY HITTING PEOPLE

OVER THE HEAD — THAT'S ASSAULT,

NOT LEADERSHIP.

Dwight D. Eisenhower

MANAGEMENT ALWAYS MEANS MEASUREMENT

"Suppose one of you wants to build a tower, will he not first sit down and estimate the cost to see if he has enough money to complete it."

Luke 14:28-32

I don't know about you, but nothing frustrates me more than starting a project and not being able to finish it. Wait... no, there is something else: my staff starting a project and not seeing it to completion!

Coming up with great ideas is never a problem within our organization. Coming up with the right idea to meet the needs of our clients is never a problem either. But having the right resources, the right people, and the right skills to see it to completion, that is sometimes a challenge.

I am a visionary by nature and I love what I do. So for me

to take on a new project is a thrill and something I enjoy. But for my organization and staff to cope with the new adventure is sometimes a challenge.

Years ago, I read this simple illustration by Jesus and developed a motto that has stood me in good stead ever since:

NO PEOPLE; NO PROJECT! OR NEW PROJECT = NEW PEOPLE!

We all agree with the concept that people are our greatest asset and our greatest resource. But often when it comes to new projects and assignments, we take the same people with the same skills and the same budgets and an established work load and then we dump on them new responsibilities and new vision and expect more from them. There is something wrong with this picture.

Jesus said, before you start any new project, assess its viability and assess its cost. We can all start things, but can we finish them? He doesn't say: have all your ducks in a row. He goes so far as to suggest that if you're going up against a warring King, an opposing business, and you are outgunned two to one — are you committed to seeing it through?

He doesn't say don't attempt the impossible, just be aware it is going to cost you!

NO PEOPLE, NO PROJECT!

WHAT'S THE BIG DEAL WITH MONEY?

"Whoever can be trusted with very little can also be trusted with much."

Luke 16:10-12

Jesus taught that our ability to handle and be wise stewards of our finances is a qualifier put in place by God to judge whether or not we are ready/able/capable of being a steward over more important things or the next level things.

One of the wealthiest men in the history of the world, King Solomon of Israel, said that poverty was the result of either stupidity or unrighteous living.

If you do a study through Solomon's writings in the Book of Proverbs and throughout the Old Testament, you will find that poverty is the result of: foolishness, unrighteousness, gambling, poor investment, wayward living, bad company, poor stewardship, laziness and not bringing in the tithe (let's call this a lack of a generous spirit).

These are not the sort of characteristics that you want to have on your leadership team.

I think it is realistic when interviewing for new positions, especially in leadership roles, to review the fiscal performance of the potential candidate. Because if someone cannot steward their own money, what makes you think that they will steward yours any better? If someone can't keep their own household budget in order, what makes you think that they will be able to manage a multi-million dollar department? Yes, you do measure grace. Yes, you do make allowance. Yes, you do offer training, but I think, especially in senior leadership positions, that this is the exception, not the rule.

Your key leaders need to come pre-qualified and one of the key indicators of their personal discipleship is the stewardship of their personal finances.

> KING SOLOMON OF ISRAEL SAID THAT POVERTY WAS THE RESULT OF EITHER STUPIDITY OR UNRIGHTEOUS LIVING.

ᏚLAP SADDLES, KNOCK HEADS AND CUT YOUR LOSSES

"If anyone will not welcome you or listen to your words, shake the dust off your feet when you leave that home or town." Matthew 10:14

There are times when you just have to get out of Dodge!

There are times when you have to admit that you just plain made a mistake. There are times when it just isn't going to work. There are times when the product is just terrible or the market is just not ready. There are times when people just aren't going to change. There are times… you get the picture.

At times like these Jesus said — just cut your losses and move on. Not everybody is going to like you. Not everybody is going to buy from you. Not every idea that you have is going to be a good idea.

It is true that nothing is ever made without making a mistake. However, nothing is gained by doing the same thing over and over again and expecting a different result. That isn't persistence, that's just dumb. Henry Ford said: Failure is an opportunity to begin again, more intelligently.

There are times when, for the sake of your bottom line and for the future of your organization, you just have to say enough is enough. Cut your losses and move on. Nothing is ever wasted, even our worst failures. You will always pay for your education; you just shouldn't have to go bankrupt doing it.

Just dust off your shoes, address an opponent, fire the offending staff member, close down the branch, stop production of the product and move on.

REMEMBER: YOU WILL ALWAYS PAY FOR YOUR EDUCATION; YOU JUST SHOULDN'T HAVE TO GO BANKRUPT DOING IT.

$\mathcal{N}$EARLY ALL MEN CAN STAND
ADVERSITY, BUT IF YOU WANT TO
TEST A MAN'S CHARACTER,
GIVE HIM POWER.

Abraham Lincoln

*T*HE QUALITY OF A PERSON'S LIFE

IS IN DIRECT PROPORTION TO THEIR

COMMITMENT TO EXCELLENCE,

REGARDLESS OF THEIR CHOSEN

FIELD OF ENDEAVOR.

Vincent T. Lombardi

$\mathcal{F}$IND A PLACE TO SERVE

"*Instead, whoever wants to become great among you must be your servant.*"

Matthew 20:26

Early on in my career, I had obtained positions of senior leadership within several organizations that I was involved in.

I remember sitting down one day and assessing who I was, where I was going and what I was responsible for.

In the process, I realized that I held the position of 'leader' in every one of the areas I was overseeing. I was not directly serving anyone; I was being served by everyone.

As life goes on and as success comes our way, it is easy to be on the receiving end of everybody's good will and kind words — you're the boss, they have to say the right thing and do the right thing. Jesus says clearly if you want to be great, you have to be prepared to serve. The desire for an impact-filled life is not a negative thing, but is something we must ensure is not achieved at another's expense. Jesus said that if we serve, we ensure not only leadership today, but longevity, fruitfulness and greatness over a lifetime.

When I realized I was not 'serving' someone else, I realized I was limiting my future. I was limiting my opportunities because I had limited my relationships and sphere of influence. An attitude of serving, like an attitude of gratitude, is contagious. Find an avenue to extend grace, find a place to serve and give a little of what has been given to you. This may be within your own organization, or in the community touched by your organization.

As you, the key leader, change your focus outward, you will start to change the culture of your organization. You will notice your staff looking beyond their own needs and their own departments. You will find your company looking beyond itself and out into the community and market place. As your corporate presence becomes a community presence, people will start to talk of the good you do, not just the products you sell. That sort of PR can't be bought!

JESUS SAID THAT IF WE SERVE WE ENSURE NOT ONLY LEADERSHIP TODAY, BUT LONGEVITY AND GREATNESS OVER A LIFETIME.

$\mathcal{T}$AKE TIME TO TEACH

"$\mathcal{A}$fter $\mathcal{J}$esus had finished instructing his twelve disciples,
$\mathcal{H}$e went on from there to teach and preach in
the towns of $\mathcal{G}$alilee." Matthew 11:1

As leadership and learning are indispensable to each other, so is leadership and teaching. You are only ever a success after you have replaced yourself with or trained a successor.

Everything Jesus did was in a public place. Everything He said and every miracle He performed was under public scrutiny. Every issue He confronted was done in the presence of His disciples. He used every occasion to teach them lessons that they would need to successfully become His successors.

Life's lessons are always best learned on the job instead of in a classroom or before a review board.

Whenever you head into the field — take someone with you. When you are going into a sticky negotiation — take someone with you. Whenever you go to lunch — take someone with you.

When faced with the tough calls, the big challenges, include those that you are training up. In these environments your staff will see the best and the worst of you and hopefully they will end up being a better version of you altogether!

Teaching and training others is not just an event, it is an attitude that says: I see beyond my current position and myself.

To actively train and teach others means that you do not see what you are currently doing as the last thing you shall ever do.

Jesus certainly didn't. He knew that one day He would be 'promoted'. He knew He was heading to a higher calling than what He was currently engaged in. With every opportunity, every day, He taught, so that when the time arose He was able to move on without a concern for those that were left to succeed Him. In fact He said — greater things than these shall you also do!

Teaching and training others says: I see the potential and possibility not only in myself, but in my staff and team.

> TEACHING AND TRAINING OTHERS IS NOT JUST AN EVENT, IT IS AN ATTITUDE THAT SAYS: I SEE BEYOND MY CURRENT POSITION AND MYSELF.

$\mathcal{G}$RATITUDE CONFIRMS RELATIONSHIPS

"I tell you the truth; the Son can do nothing by Himself." John 5:19

Words have tremendous power. You create your world with the power of your words. You can create a world of intimacy and trust just by saying 'thank you' and 'you are appreciated.'

Life and death are held in the power of our tongue. We can bring life or bring death to situations, people and possibilities all with the same little organ — the tongue!

The biggest thing you can do for sound ongoing staff and personal relationships is attach a card, a phone message or a public notice of thanks for the effort and the impact of another's achievements. We often look for big things to do to reward our staff and affirm their efforts. By all means you should do these things. But make sure that you are not hiding behind the gift.

You can create an atmosphere of mistrust and resentment simply by carelessly overlooking the efforts and achievements of your team members. Remember that what is appreciated gains value, but what depreciates loses value. It is as true of cars and real estate as it is of relationships.

Appreciate others and your value as well as theirs increases.

Neglect the small, overlook the little, and you will find that you have created an environment of assumption, not appreciation and value.

> REMEMBER THAT WHAT APPRECIATES GAINS VALUE, BUT WHAT DEPRECIATES LOSES VALUE.

PROSPERITY IS ONLY AN INSTRUMENT TO BE USED, NOT A DEITY TO BE WORSHIPPED.

Calvin Coolidge

OUR BUSINESS IN LIFE IS NOT TO GET

AHEAD OF OTHERS, BUT TO GET AHEAD

OF OURSELVES — TO BREAK OUR OWN

RECORDS, TO OUTSTRIP OUR

YESTERDAY BY OUR TODAY.

Stewart B. Johnson

CHOOSE YOUR KEY STAFF

" 'Come follow me,' Jesus said."

Mark 1:17

An inherited team is no team at all.

With any new adventure, you have to have the team you need and the team you are confident of in order to pursue the plan that is on your heart.

Jesus chose His own staff, each brought a different skill, each had a different passion, each was necessary for the long-term success of His mission

It is true that Judas did betray Him. Jesus was responsible for providing the opportunity; Judas was responsible for his life choices and actions. Jesus saw the potential in Judas, but Judas didn't take time to see the big picture. The lesson here is that you will never get all of your staff selections right. But you are better off having to live with your choices than live with the choices imposed on you by others.

If you employ a new middle manager, always do so with the understanding that they will want to and should have the right to reshuffle the deck to build a team that they can be responsible for the performance of — for better or worse.

If you come into a new position or take over a new company, I would suggest you go ahead and put everyone on notice immediately.

That gives you a sense of control, them a way out if they feel they need it, and the whole organization a chance to merge into a new entity. There is nothing worse than trying to achieve the impossible and having to butt up with the unworkable.

AN INHERITED TEAM IS NO TEAM AT ALL.

PRAISE IN PUBLIC, REBUKE IN PRIVATE

"But He said to them, 'why are you fearful, O you of little faith.'" Matthew 8:26

Often, there were times that Jesus had to challenge his disciples in the training process. Although we are privy to these conversations, they were not done in a public setting.

He celebrated the return of the 70, saying that "Greater things than these shall be done."

He applauded the faith of the woman with the issue of blood in front of the crowd; He spoke admiringly to the centurion concerning his faith for his daughter. Yet in the situations that need the strongest attention, the firmest correction concerning the action of His Inner Twelve, He did it in private.

He challenged Judas quietly as he sat beside Him at the Last Supper. He went to Peter privately on the beach after Peter betrayed Him. He pulled them aside and challenged their lack of faith, lack of ability to hear, see or understand. While sitting in a boat, He challenged their attention and understanding of His teaching.

Jesus never had a problem with confronting the lack of understanding that His disciples had. He always used their errors or their lack of knowledge as a way of teaching them, instructing them and of bettering them. But He never used their ignorance as a weapon to wound. He used His insight as a tool for equipping and training.

His desire to see His people grow was based on His concern and passion to see them become all that they could become. He rebuked them because He cared for them and wanted to help them, not hurt and humiliate them.

> HE NEVER USED THEIR IGNORANCE AS A WEAPON TO WOUND. BUT USED HIS INSIGHT AS A TOOL FOR EQUIPPING.

COMMUNICATION ENCOURAGES COMMITMENT

"For which of you, intending to build a tower, does not sit down first and count the cost, whether he has enough to finish." Luke 14:28

In any growing organization there is a need for a commitment to a vision over and above the ordinary 9 to 5. What I have found is that the worst thing you can do with any new growth or expansion program is under-communicate how much time and energy it is going to cost to get the job done.

Jesus never sugar-coated what the cost of establishing His kingdom would be to His disciples. He constantly challenged them to assess the cost, pay the price and to be aware of what others' reaction to them would be. This didn't discourage them; in fact, it increased their commitment to the cause. They had years to think about it, process it, and get their families used to the idea.

And still they sold their life out to it because He made them part of the process and not a victim of it.

You will find that people are only ever committed to what they will confess. If you can't articulate the vision of the organization, how can you expect others to commit to it?

Conversely, once you start to hear others clearly confess the core values and your corporate goals as a part of their every day life, you know that they are committed to seeing them through. As the deadline approaches for the implementation of the new program or project, listen to the confession of your people and you will be able to gauge their commitment and identify where the possible problems lie. Because what's in a person will always eventually come out if you listen long enough.

Jesus taught that out of the abundance, the overflow of the heart, the mouth speaks. Sometimes it is best not to rebuke someone for being negative, but just simply address the fear behind the negativity.

If you target your in-house communications to address the issues opposed by the confession of your employees, you will notice a change. First in their heads, then in their hearts and then out of their mouths. Generational faith means that you take your family with you into your destiny. It means that your great grandchildren, whom you may never meet, will continue the vision. Jacob never met Abraham, but fulfilled his dream. You business goals or church goals or personal goals should and must be a focus, but never at the expense of your family.

Just like you communicate with your staff and team, learn to communicate with your spouse and children about the road ahead and the price that needs to be paid to accomplish what becomes shared goals.

It is always an easier path to travel if you start with open communication. If your communication is open at the beginning then you can talk and make adjustments as you journey along... together.

> YOU WILL ALWAYS FIND THAT EFFECTIVE
> COMMUNICATION BRINGS INCREASED
> COMMITMENT.

*G*ood communication is as
stimulating as black coffee and
just as hard to sleep after.

Anne Morrow Lindbergh

$\mathcal{A}$RE THEY 'GOOD TO GO?'

*"The Lord appointed seventy others also, and
sent them out two by two."*

Luke 10:1

$\mathbf{M}$anagement by delegation is essential to all growing organizations and is a sign of mature, secure leadership. Management by neglect, however, is more often what is practiced.

Jesus had trained His men, raised His men, equipped His men, but He also tested His men. On more than one occasion He sent them out to conduct their own 'field tests'. He gave them very specific assignments, with very specific goals and very predictable outcomes. He wanted to see how they would measure up in the real world — whether or not they could be responsible with the 'power' that He was giving them.

God never gives authority without accountability, and

neither should we. The greater the responsibility, the greater the accountability must be. Jesus sent the disciples out two by two and the results were wonderful.

Luke recalls that the trainees were ecstatic with the results. They had exceeded their own expectations, let alone what they believed Jesus wanted of them.

From this platform of self-assuredness, Jesus was able to lift their vision to the greater things that they would accomplish in the time to come. He used this to encourage them to see beyond themselves to a legacy that would touch the world.

> THE GREATER THE RESPONSIBILITY, THE
> GREATER THE ACCOUNTABILITY
> MUST BE.

$\mathcal{S}$AY IT MORE THAN ONCE

"The kingdom of Heaven is like..."
Matthew 13:31

Jesus often said the same thing different ways. "The Kingdom of God is...:

* Like a mustard seed
* Like scattered seed
* Like small children
* Is coming
* Is here
* Is a mystery hidden in parables
* Is near
* Is within you

He was presenting different facets of the same concept in different ways to different people. Everybody is wired differently. You show an inkblot to 10 different people and you get 10 different interpretations.

Effective communication means that what you say and what is heard are the same thing. And most of the time it isn't! So you have to say it over and over again in different creative ways to ensure that different people with different paradigms get the same message.

Effective communication IS NOT a one-off memo and a full color corporate vision statement; it is an ongoing commitment to getting everyone on the same page.

Effective communication is saying with passion and integrity the same message over and over until everybody that has ears to hear — hears!

> EFFECTIVE COMMUNICATION IS SAYING WITH PASSION AND INTEGRITY THE SAME MESSAGE UNTIL EVERYBODY HEARS IT.

$\mathcal{G}$IVE HONOR WHERE HONOR IS DUE

"$\mathcal{R}$ender therefore to $\mathcal{C}$aesar the things that are $\mathcal{C}$aesar's, and to $\mathcal{G}$od the things that are $\mathcal{G}$od's."

$\mathcal{L}$uke 20:25

Throughout His life, Jesus was constantly making reference to the Father and giving thanks to the Father. He gave honor where honor was due.

In business there is a tendency to 'blow your own trumpet — because no one else will'. A healthy view of yourself and your achievements is not a problem. In fact, Paul said it is a useful thing to boast on occasion. He even said it was something that some people needed to hear. But the higher principle is to make sure you are not laying claim to the achievements of other team members.

Jesus had no problem with the ambition of His team

members; He just made sure that they understood that you didn't aspire to leadership at the expense of others, but as a result of serving others, and He always gave honor where honor was due. And He always gave honor where honor was due.

Just as you can steal things, you can steal honor. A team effort is just that — a TEAM effort. It is not their effort and your accolades. It took a team to accomplish it and a team should benefit from it. Actively find platforms from which to give praise.

By giving honor where honor is due, you gain your team's respect, their loyalty, and their commitment to other projects and to your organization.

> ## ACTIVELY FIND PLATFORMS FROM WHICH TO GIVE PRAISE.

MEN OCCASIONALLY STUMBLE OVER
THE TRUTH, BUT MOST OF THEM PICK
THEMSELVES UP AND HURRY OFF AS IF
NOTHING EVER HAPPENED.

Sir Winston Churchill

PRINCIPLES
OF LONGEVITY

*P*ASSION IS THE QUICKEST TO

DEVELOP, AND THE QUICKEST TO FADE.

INTIMACY DEVELOPS MORE SLOWLY,

AND COMMITMENT MORE

GRADUALLY STILL.

Robert Sternberg

Say WHAT YOU MEAN AND DO WHAT YOU SAY

"But let your yes be yes and your no, no."

Matthew 5:37

The true gauge of a person's character is not given in a handshake or a signature on a contract, but when they give their word.

We trust God because we trust His Word. He said He never lies. He said His Word is true. The Bible says that He watches over His word to perform it. When we neglect to watch over our word, when we neglect to follow through on what we have committed to, we are doing more than just neglecting or forgetting something, we are revealing something about our true selves.

When you believe in someone, or trust someone, you are doing more than just believing in who they are. The essence of that trust is traced back to the fact that you believe in what they say — you just trust their word.

The concept of "your word is your bond" was something that Jesus was trying to drive into the hearts of a group of people that had reduced their life to laws and legalism, to claims and counter-claims, to sects and division. He was saying "Hey, let's get back to the basics here: Commandment #9 says don't lie. So why don't we cut all the garbage out and just get back to doing what we say we will do. And if you won't do what you say you'll do — then don't say it!"

To be duplicitous means to be deceptive, dishonest or misleading. There is no such thing as a 'little white lie'.

God's Word is His bond, the expression of His nature, and the measure of His character. So is ours.

> GOD'S WORD IS HIS BOND, THE EXPRESSION OF HIS NATURE THE MEASURE OF HIS CHARACTER.

$\mathcal{I}$NTEGRITY — TRUE TO WHAT SELF?

"$\mathcal{B}$ut he, knowing their hypocrisy, said to them,
'why do you test me?'"

$\mathcal{M}$ark 12:15

One day a group who opposed Christ came to Him to try to trick Him into moral duplicity based upon their own corruption. They thought their greatest weakness would also be His.

Their question wasn't based upon a genuine need to know or an area of concern in the Scripture, they hoped that in Jesus' desire to get His message out, He would try to curry favour amongst a people who were experiencing double taxation and military oppression.

But Jesus did what only Jesus could do — be true to Himself. He comforted and confounded them with the simple illustration.

When faced with advice, opportunity or even the desire to

fudge figures, or lie, your second response needs to be why? You know your reaction. You've seen the condition of your heart. So what is in you that would allow you to even contemplate this action?

Having integrity means to be true to oneself.

If you are a liar by nature, and you lie, then you are being true to yourself. If you find it easy to steal, and you steal, then in the literal sense, you are a person of integrity, because you are being true to yourself.

Our true nature is fallen and sinful. The key to change is to try not to be true to ourselves but be true to Himself, to be true to the nature of Christ. The only way we can have integrity to the teachings of Christ is to know the teachings of Christ. To allow His word to change, direct and correct our walk.

Holiness is an external evidence of an internal work. Holiness is not what you say, do or dress; that is culture more often than not. However if you change on the inside, it will be seen by the entire world on the outside.

> HOLINESS IS AN EXTERNAL EVIDENCE
> OF AN INTERNAL WORK.

$\mathcal{D}$ON'T SELL YOUR SOUL

"For what will it profit a man if he gains the whole world, and loses his soul?"

Mark 8:36

What price do you put on those things dearest to you? How much do you think something that is priceless is worth? How much is your integrity worth? How much value do you place on a reputation that takes a lifetime to build yet can be destroyed with one stupid selfish action? The spouse you have, the children you raised, how much would you be prepared to trade them for?

Every day I see people selling themselves short. Trading their future for the quick gratification of the flesh and then spending all their emotion energy trying to justify why they have done what they have done. Self-justification is always the end product of self-righteousness.

Jesus taught that there is something that money can't buy. He said that there were things deep in the heart of a person, their very core, that were worth more than all the money in the world. In fact, He went so far as to say... what would it profit you if you gain it all yet lose your soul, the core of who you are along the way?

To compromise means to settle for less than what something is really valued at. When you compromise on your ethics, your values and your commitments, you may gain materially in the short term but at the end of the day, it will cost you, it always costs you.

If you make a truce with compromise, you will always live in misery.

IF YOU MAKE A TRUCE WITH COMPROMISE, YOU WILL ALWAYS LIVE IN MISERY.

DRIVE THY BUSINESS OR IT WILL DRIVE THEE.

Benjamin Franklin

THE IDEALS WHICH HAVE ALWAYS SHONE
BEFORE ME AND FILLED ME WITH THE
JOY OF LIVING ARE GOODNESS,
BEAUTY, AND TRUTH.
TO MAKE A GOAL OF COMFORT OR
HAPPINESS HAS NEVER APPEALED TO ME;
A SYSTEM OF ETHICS BUILT ON THIS
BASIS WOULD BE SUFFICIENT
ONLY FOR A HERD
OF CATTLE.

Albert Einstein

DUNG HAPPENS!

"Lord, let it alone this year also, till I shall dig it and dung it."

Luke 13:8

Have you ever had the feeling that things aren't going your way? Have you ever felt like your year just got worse? The reaction so many have is to turn around and blame the devil. But that's not what Jesus taught. He teaches in the book of Luke that in order to bring about increased fruitfulness, you have to add fertilizer.

Jesus tells an incredible story about a very persistent steward. A steward who saw the value in a tree. A steward who insisted that the tree's true potential had not been reached. A steward who felt the best strategy to see growth was to upset the roots of the tree, put it under a little stress, fertilize it and then see it mature from its roots.

Dung happens. The fertilizer of life. The refuse. The ugly,

unattractive stuff. Take some stress; add some unsettling and uprooting, and you don't have a recipe for disaster, but an opportunity for growth and success.

God has the incredible ability to turn all things around for the good of those that love Him. Champions don't look at what they are going through, but what they are going to.

This may be a year where all you smell is the fertilizer of today's circumstances. But next year, you could very well be enjoying the sweet smell of success.

> THIS MAYBE A YEAR WHERE ALL YOU SMELL IS THE FERTILIZER OF TODAY'S CIRCUMSTANCES. BUT NEXT YEAR YOU COULD VERY WELL BE SMELLING THE SWEET SMELL OF SUCCESS.

$\mathcal{Y}$OUR SIN WILL FIND YOU OUT!

"For there's nothing covered that will not be revealed."

Luke 12:2

The 1970s was the decade of 'Me'. This lead to the 80s, which was the decade of greed. Which lead to the 90s, which was the decade of corruption. Which lead to 2000s which was the decade of revelation — they got caught!

It doesn't matter how big or how small your misdemeanor is, at sometime in the future, what people think they have gotten away with in secret will eventually be exposed.

Maybe a colleague will tell. Maybe your spouse will discover it. Maybe you will be so overcome with grief one day you will confess it. Maybe your body will grow sick and old before its time, your guilt eating you up from the inside out. But be assured — it will manifest. In all our interpersonal relationships, keep short accounts.

Paul encouraged us to wherever possible be on good terms with others. If you think this is a silly notion, think of it as a good future business investment.

We all know the world is getting smaller and the higher you rise, the less people there are filling the top position. So at some point in time, the person you ticked off or ripped off is going to end up across the table from you. Instead of having an ally, you now have an enemy.

Remember that whatever small satisfaction it brings you now, it will taste bitter at some point in the future. All seeds sown, for good or for bad, reap a harvest. All sin committed has a consequence. All actions hidden will eventually be exposed.

As in the negative, also the positive. The sins of some people are obvious and go ahead of them to judgement, but the sins of others follow afterwards. Likewise with good deeds: some you see right off, but none stay hidden forever.

> ALL SEEDS SOWN, FOR GOOD OR FOR BAD,
> REAP A HARVEST.

$\mathcal{D}$O, SHOW, TEACH

"And He marvelled because of their unbelief."

Mark 6:7

In any organization, as a developing leader you must allow yourself and indeed plan, not only for your own personal growth, but for the growth of those working with you.

Jesus was always teaching. Every opportunity He would use as a chance to pass on the 'whys' behind the 'whats' that He did.

The Psalms say that the children of Israel knew of God's acts, but Moses knew of His ways.

An employee will only ever know what to do, but an employer will always know why. You position yourself and your future through this knowledge. Never settle for knowing what, always seek the knowing why.

Jesus' teaching style was very simple: He first did; Then He showed; Then He taught.

He first did a miracle, for example, the turning of water into wine. He then allowed them to participate in a miracle, the feeding of the five thousand. He then sent them out 2 by 2 to do their own miracles. And the result? They came back excited because they had started to be an active part of the solution.

Don't be vague or general in your assignments to your team; give them clear, measurable performance indicators. Before they go, share your victories and the lessons from your failures. This way when they encounter either one of those, they will be better equipped to handle them.

Remember:

* Let them see you do 'it.'
* Show them how to do 'it.'
* Watch them do 'it.'
* Give them feedback on their performance.

> AN EMPLOYEE WILL ONLY EVER KNOW WHAT TO DO, BUT AN EMPLOYER WILL ALWAYS KNOW WHY.

DEFINE YOUR BUSINESS GOALS CLEARLY

SO THAT OTHERS CAN SEE

THEM AS YOU DO.

George F. Burns

WE GO WHERE OUR VISION IS.

Joseph Murphy

$\mathcal{W}$HEN FACED WITH UNETHICAL BEHAVIOR, DEAL WITH IT ONCE, FIRMLY AND PUBLICLY.

"Then Jesus went into the temple and began to drive out those who bought and sold."

Mark 11:15

Jesus was faced with what had become a culture of corruption in the temple of His Father. The exchanging of money was originally established to help in the worship of God; it had now become an avenue for corruption and religious extortion. It had moved from the core values and practices of the original plan.

Jesus knew about the practice all His life. But when the right time came, He dealt with it once firmly, publicly and with no room for misinterpretation.

When dealing with unethical practices in the business arena, consider the following as a guideline for action:

* Have all your facts together. Jesus knew exactly what was going on and how it deviated from the original plan.
* Deal with a public wrong, publicly. He exposed the wrongdoing for what it really was.
* As the leader, there will be repercussions to your reputation — cowboy up and get it done. Jesus didn't try to protect His Father's reputation. He knew that in order to address the culture of unethical behavior, everybody had to know where He stood and what He stood for.
* Deal with it swiftly. Jesus didn't discuss it or form a committee on the issue. All His thinking and planning had been done previously, now was the time for execution.
* He was fully aware of the consequences of his actions and was prepared for the long-term gain from what was a short-term unpopular action.

When cutting out the cancer of unethical behavior, cosmetic surgery is no replacement for the radical surgery that is needed to address the issue. Cosmetic surgery may cover it up, but the damage will continue to rot and fester beneath the surface. The result: *Infection and death.*

> HE KNEW THAT IN ORDER TO ADDRESS THE CULTURE OF UNETHICAL BEHAVIOR, EVERYBODY HAD TO KNOW WHERE HE STOOD.

ℰTHICS ARE NOT CIRCUMSTANTIAL

"But let your yes be yes and your no, no."
Mark 5:37

In an era of moving morality and self-serving justice, the teaching of Jesus concerning ethics is a stark contrast. "Let your yes, be yes and your no, no." Simple really, easy to understand, not open to interpretation, absolute!

Lack of absolutes within our community and our corporate world has lead to the erosion of our morality and will ultimately affect our government and our economy just as they have our churches.

Riches obtained based upon a lie will only ever last for a season. Prosperity that has grown out of truth, will last a lifetime.

You must insist on a stand of absolutes from your self, from your staff and then from those around you. What is right is right and what is wrong is wrong. And there is nothing but a sharp dividing line between them.

It may not make you popular at first, but you'll never be caught hanging your head in shame on the cover of a national newspaper or hiding under a blanket on the 6 o'clock news.

IN AN ERA OF MOVING MORALITY AND SELF-SERVING JUSTICE, THE TEACHING OF JESUS CONCERNING ETHICS IS A STARK CONTRAST.

$\mathcal{I}$T'S ALL ABOUT CHARACTER

" $\mathcal{Y}$ou were faithful over a few things, $\mathcal{I}$ will make you ruler over many things."

Matthew 25:21

The job of being 'The Messiah' was not something you applied for with a resume to the Employment office. It was something that Jesus walked towards all His life. He didn't do the job, He was the job.

Your destiny is not something you do, it's someone you become. Don't build your career around your reputation, but around your character. Character is portable, your reputation is not. You take your character from job to job; your reputation stays with your relationships.

Others can ruin your reputation, only you can ruin your character. Jesus promised that when we have been faithful in little He will give us much. He promised that when we have been faithful with another's vision, with another's business, He will give us our own.

Faithfulness is the bedrock of character. All leadership is limited by the worth of their character and the extent of their knowledge. Both of these are things you develop; they are not things you simply 'do'.

The business scandals of the last few years have reinforced one thing over and over again. Ed Cole would often tell me that you always pay the highest price for the lowest form of living.

* The death penalty is the price for murder.
* Addiction is the price for drug use.
* Divorce and a shattered family is the price for adultery.
* Missed opportunity and unfulfilled dreams are the price of an unteachable spirit and an undisciplined mind.

The decisions of our destiny are not made publicly, but made privately, in the quiet places of 'small' temptations.

> THE DECISIONS OF OUR DESTINY ARE NOT MADE PUBLICLY, BUT MADE PRIVATELY, IN THE 'QUIET' PLACES OF 'SMALL' TEMPTATIONS.

$\mathcal{Y}$OU CANNOT DREAM YOURSELF INTO
A CHARACTER; YOU MUST HAMMER
AND FORGE YOURSELF ONE.

James A. Froude

WHEN THE CHARACTER OF A MAN
IS NOT CLEAR TO YOU, LOOK
AT HIS FRIENDS.

Japanese Proverb

$\mathcal{T}$HE LOVE OF MONEY IS MORE THAN JUST DOLLARS AND CENTS

"$\mathcal{N}$o servant can serve two masters."

$\mathcal{L}$uke 16:13

$\mathcal{M}$ammon was originally a Syrian word for the term money. This was its everyday use at the time of Christ. But Jesus noticed that there had crept into the life of the Pharisees a change in their attitude towards money. He noticed that they had stop serving God with mammon and had started to love mammon as God.

Jesus noticed that this attitude was affecting every aspect of their lives. It made them arrogant (Luke 16:15), it divided their focus and their affections (Luke 16:13), it made them unfaithful (Luke 16:13), it made them envious of others (Luke 12:15), they no longer had compassion and they had become obsessed with pretence and public acceptance and social standing (Luke 20:47).

The love of money extends far beyond the simple desire to acquire cash. It really has little to do with a person's desire to do well in life and more about who we see as our source.

The most effective way to judge your attitude toward money is to ask yourself: in crisis, whom do I run to first?: Medicare or Scripture? Do I tithe based on my bank balance or my commitment to God? Is my word my bond or something that I give freely and keep loosely? Do I listen to correction from a friend or do I treat all relationships like disposable items?

All of these things indicate a heart's attitude to the core values of the teachings of Christ. You can serve God with mammon (money) but you can't serve Mammon and God. One is about God and the other is about self.

The satisfaction of self is the preoccupation of a sin-filled world and a broken-down church. So many Christians want the abundant life promised by Jesus without the Lordship that is involved.

When I was first married, I was taught that money and sex are for loving and giving, not lusting and getting. That love is about satisfying others at the expense of self, because love desires to give, whereas lust is about satisfying self at the expense of others, because lust desires to get.

You should see money as a tool and God as your source. If you do this, then every area of your life will prosper.

> YOU CAN SERVE GOD WITH MAMMON —MONEY—
> BUT YOU CAN'T SERVE GOD AND MAMMON.

WEALTH AND RICHES

"For where your treasure is, there your heart is also."

Matthew 6:19-21

Our western culture does not differentiate between wealth and riches. In fact, we believe that you need riches to be wealthy.

The truth is, it's the other way around. If you don't have wealth, you'll never have lasting riches. Riches are "perishable assets" which Christ warned us not to improperly focus on as the primary goal of our labor.

Riches can be gained initially without ethics and morals. Wealth, on the other hand, is primarily achieved through the skills, spiritual knowledge and character developed in obeying God's ways in resource management.

* Riches are something we HAVE
* Wealth is someone we ARE

If you take riches off a rich person, they will become poor. If you take riches off of a wealthy person, they will never be impoverished, they will simply be without money for a while.

Wealthy people will always overcome their crisis for cash because they are wealthy. The morally bankrupt will always stay bankrupt, regardless of how much money they have.

> # RICHES ARE SOMETHING WE HAVE.
> # WEALTH IS SOMEONE WE ARE.

$\mathcal{M}$EN MAKE HISTORY, AND NOT
THE OTHER WAY AROUND. IN PERIODS
WHERE THERE IS NO LEADERSHIP, SOCIETY
STANDS STILL. PROGRESS OCCURS WHEN
COURAGEOUS, SKILLFUL LEADERS SEIZE
THE OPPORTUNITY TO CHANGE
THINGS FOR THE BETTER.

Harry S. Truman

$\mathcal{A}$ REFLECTION FOR YOU

$\mathcal{A}$s with all of life our destinies are not based upon
circumstances, but based upon decisions.

Destiny is not about what you do, but about who you become.

Following Christ is not about religion, but about a divine
connection and acknowledgement that He is who He says
He is and can do what He says He can do.

As John Ashcroft said: It is an issue of Kingship.
Who is Lord over our nation and our life?

*Unique among the nations, America recognized the source of our
character as being godly and eternal, not being civic and temporal.
And because we have understood that our source is eternal,
America has been different. We have no king but Jesus.*

*John Ashcroft
Attorney General, United States of America.*

$\mathcal{A}$ STATEMENT FOR YOU

"...people often say about Him: "I'm ready to accept Jesus
as a great moral teacher, but I don't accept His claim to
be God." That is the one thing we must not say.

A man who was merely a man and said the sort of things Jesus
said would not be a great moral teacher. He would either be a
lunatic — on a level with the man who says he is a poached
egg — or else he would be the Devil of Hell.

You must make your choice.

Either this man was, and is, the Son of God: or else a
madman or something worse.

You can shut Him up for a fool, you can spit at Him and kill
Him as a demon; or you can fall at His feet and call Him
Lord and God.

But let us not come with any patronizing nonsense about
His being a great human teacher.

He has not left that open to us. He did not intend to."

C. S. Lewis

About the Author

John King; is a prominent, gregarious, sought-after conference, business & church speaker. He is usually characterized by friends & colleagues as one of the most powerful & passionate speakers on leadership, men's and value based issues.

John's impact as a communicator is far reaching. He has touched people all over the world through corporate seminars, television shows & his books. He is the author of the best selling books Now to Next — Blueprint for a Church Revolution; It's a Guy Thing; Manhood, Marriage and Family; Raising Messiah — The Life of the Most Influential Stepfather in History and now, Business By The Book — Leadership and Management Principles from the Life of Christ.

He and his wife, Beccy, founded the International Men's Network and have overseen its growth & development personally. The International Men's Network has offices in 30 nations around the world.

They also founded the Next Foundation, a Christian missionary organization, that is dedicated to helping prepare leaders for the coming age.

Books & Teachings

BY JOHN KING

Now to Next — Blueprint for a Church revolution
Now to Next — The Study Guide
It's a Guy Thing — Manhood, Marriage and Family
Original Thought — Reflections on the journey so far
Rasing Messiah — Lessons from the world's most
influential stepfather.

John's numerous teaching series on both DVD and CD
are available in our online catalogue at
WWW.IMNONLINE.ORG

Contact Information

International Men's Network
Head Office: +1-817-993-0047 Fax: +1-817-898-0217
PO Box 827 Roanoke, 76262 Texas USA
Email: info@imnonline.org
WWW.IMNONLINE.ORG

Printed in the United States
50919LVS00002B/1-15